The S●UL
of A Poet
He'll Blow Your Mind With His Poetry Lines

The S●UL of A Poet

He'll Blow Your Mind With His Poetry Lines

Written by Ronald Marsh Smith

Cover art by Ben L. Gillette

COPYRIGHT

Copyright © 2019 by Ronald Marsh Smith.

All rights reserved. This book or any portion thereof may not be reproduced or used in any manner whatsoever without the express written permission of Ronald Marsh Smith and Butterfly Typeface Publishing except for the use of brief quotations in a book review.

Printed in the United States of America

First Printing, 2019

ISBN [Hardback]: 978-1-947656-91-8

ISBN [Paperback]: 978-1-947656-86-4

Library of Congress Number: 2018957722

The Butterfly Typeface Publishing
PO Box 56193
Little Rock AR 72215

www.thebutterflytypeface.com

there is Soul Food

there is Soul Music

there is Soul Brother

there is Soul Sister

there is Spiritual Soul

there are Soulmates

and then there is....

The Soul of A Poet

He'll blow your mind with his poetry lines!

DEDICATION

This work, *The Soul of a Poet*, is the reflection of a lesson I learned early and one that I have tried to share throughout my life - the importance of the choice(s) one makes in life.

A woman I never knew, my mother, was violated and raped. She passed away when I was two years old.

In my mind, GOD spoke to her and said, "Ella, keep your darling son, and through him, your Victory will be won."

Without her choice, there would be no me!

Thank you, Mother.

I love you!

Photo 1 Ella L. Smith | 1929-1961

TABLE OF CONTENTS

Preface 23
Loud And Bold 25
    Don't Look Down on Me 26
    I Stare 27
    Jail 28
    Stained Glass 29
    Wondering 30
    Your Book 31

Stories To Be Told 33
    A Family Christmas 34
    Christmas Time 35
    Thanksgiving 36
    Merry Christmas Baby 38
    Merry Christmas My Dear 39

Feelings Of Fire 41
    Do My 42
    Last Night 43
    Pretty Lady 44
    Your Eyes 45
    Passion for You 46

Truth And Desire 47

    Black Diamond 48

    From My Heart 49

    I Dream 50

    If I Could 51

    Love Is 52

    Planting Love 53

Wisdom And Truth 55

    Dear Lord.. 56

    Heaven Isn't Free 57

    How Much Do I Owe You 59

    Master 60

    No Grave 61

    Nobody Know... 62

    When Morning Come....................................... 63

Attention To Youth... 65

    Children of the Night.. 66

    Don't Have A Clue.. 67

    Dreaming.. 69

    I have Autism 70

    Stop the Bullying 71

    We Too Exist.. 73

    What Do You See 75

Built-Up Wall 77
    Fight With Cancer 78
    A Glimpse of Tomorrow 79
    A Smile 80
    A View Of Life 81
    Difficulties 82
    Down But Not Out 83
    I am a Slave 84
    Kindness 85
    Tomorrow 86
    Troubled 87

Before You Fall 89
    Buried in the Atlantic Ocean 90
    End This Way 92
    Help Me 93
    Life 94
    Live Life 95
    Troubling Times 96
    Vows Broken 98

Eyes Shut Tight 101
    At Peace 102
    Bruno 103
    Cam 105

I Am Free	107
Miss You Sis	110
My Brother	112
She's With You	114
The Mighty Nine	116

Pillow On A Troubled Night 119

Always Love You	120
Cried My Last Tears	121
Lies of Love	122
Remember	123
Time	125
Wish	126

Whatever You Want It To Be 127

Mona's Yarn	128
My Final Day	130
No Roses	132
Your Calling	133
Your Marriage	135

Deeply Rooted In Poetry 137

A Daddy's Message	138
A Mother's Kiss	140
Family Reunion	142
Family & Friends	144

Single Mother 146
Epilogue.. 149
For My Husband 151
For My Wife 153
The Soul of A Poet (Author's Biography) 155
A Note From The Publisher 169

FOREWORD

Master Sergeant, Ronald Smith (Retired U.S. Army), a man and once an Army Soldier, is a man whom I have had the great pleasure of serving with and knowing for over twenty years.

His fascinating new book of poems, The Soul of A Poet, is the result of a vision embedded in him for many years and has now come to fruition in the form of publication.

Ronald shared his dream with me during our military tour in South Korea at Camp Red Cloud, where I was his Senior Non-Commissioned Officer. As we carried out our military duties, he shared some of his writings/poems with me. As I read these poems, they moved me (my mind went back to yesterday, the old school ways - you know what I mean) and I hope they also compel you to think about yesterday's love, failures, and accomplishments that we all have experienced in life.

One of the most memorable poems written by this great man was for the Pace, Chieves and McRae Family, titled "Family Reunion." Read it, and I think you'll agree with me that it is an awesome poem.

During Ronald's hardship through life, he never lost sight of his strong belief in God and his dedication to writing and his creative ability in expressing his true feelings in the form of poetry.

When I received a phone call from my dear friend and listened to him tell me that he had found a publisher for his poems, I didn't know who was more excited, him or me. Not only is Ronald a great friend, who served our country with honor and distinction, but he was also a true military warrior.

The hopes I had years ago for this great poet are finally realized. I wish him great success now and in his future writings.

Ronald, continue to write and move forward with God as your pilot. The path to greater success is paved for you.

Readers, pour yourself a glass of your favorite wine, sit back and reconnect your mind. Allow your thoughts to travel back in time to the romance and even the broken hearts of yesterday's love.

One of the greatest joys in life is the ability to recall what once was and what could be.

Enjoy!

Marvin L. Pace

Sergeant Major, U.S. Army, Retired

Acknowledgments

This project would not have been possible without the encouragement and support of the many people I met throughout my lifetime. First, it gives me great joy in acknowledging God - the Alpha and the Omega, the beginning and the end. The mountains God gave me the strength to climb, from an early age, are what have made this book a reality. Hebrews 13:5, says I will never leave you, nor will I forsake you.

A profound thank you, wrapped with unconditional love is extended to my birth mother, a mother I never had the pleasure of knowing. Despite her situation of being violated by a stranger, she found an abundance of love in her heart to give me life and keep me. She's my hero! I want to also thank my foster parents who opened their homes and hearts and for bringing stability into my life.

I would like to take this opportunity to offer a gracious *thank you* and *much love* to my phenomenal wife, Betty, and my three wonderful sons: Ronald Jr., Raymond Sr., and Ryan. To my grandchildren, I pray this collection of poetry will be an inspiration in your life. To my daughters-in-law, you have grown to be more like daughters. My wife and I are blessed to have you in our family. To all of my relatives, my sisters and brother, I thank God we are blessed to share a DNA that has engulfed us with the pillar of faith, love, and strength.

Thank you, Rev. George O. Stewart, Zion Chapel Baptist Church, Cleveland, Ohio, whose spiritual direction brought me through the darkest hours of my early army career. Thank you to the late Corrine E. Berry and the entire Lee Harvard community for their prayers.

I want to also thank Charles Lee for being a father figure and mentor to me when I had no father figure in my life. The words "Thank You" aren't enough to repay you for the invaluable one-on-one conversations, mentorship and support throughout the many years. You were and still today are an inspiration to me. Thank You!

Now to Command Sergeant Major (Retired) Anthony L. Rucci; as my First Sergeant, despite the problems I endured during the early stage of my military service, under your leadership you taught me how to be a **"Come Back Soldier."** Through your molding and one on one counseling, I learned how to "Make That Dog Hunt." Thank You!

To Command Sergeant Major Gavin Tunderman (Retired), wow, thirty-seven years of friendship that began in 1981 as Cadre at Basic Leadership Course (BLC), at Emery Barracks, Wurzburg, Germany. Thank you for showing me the ropes, how to be an effective Tactical Sergeant and Instructor. "Can't touch Salt & Pepper." "HOOAH."

Sound Attention: To Sergeant Major (Retired) Marvin L. Pace, I want to personally thank you for your never-ending words of encouragement. Whenever I send you a new creation, you say, "I love the poem, now when are you going to get these poems in a book?" Well, Sergeant Major, mission accomplished!

I would be remiss if I didn't send a special *Shout Out* to Bertheria and Felicia Gaston. Thank you for all of your invaluable assistance.

And to Patricia Moss, Clarksville, Tennessee, for always asking me, "Have you written anything new?" and giving me words of encouragement to keep writing.

Space doesn't allow me to acknowledge my dearest friends whom I've known over the many years and all my fellow comrades in arms I have had the distinct pleasure of serving with during my 21 years of military service. A "BIG" thank you to all of you. Now to my extended family, 226/229th Supply & Service Company, Wilkins Barracks, Germany (1988-1991), never did I imagine you of all people would have such love for your "Hardcore" Platoon Sergeant (PSG). Thank you! Remember, "Hardcore Soldiers Never Die, When They're Shot, They Never Cry."

Last, but not least, I want to thank Iris M. Williams and the team at Butterfly Typeface Publishing. Thanks for your leadership, creativity, innovation, patience and unwavering support. You and your staff have made *The Soul of a Poet* come to fruition.

The Soul of A Poet

His soul resounds loud and bold,

with *a many* stories to be told.

His soul emits feelings of fire,

holding truth and desire.

His soul speaks wisdom and truth,

and can grab the attention of the youth.

His soul can tear down your built-up wall,

and can catch you before you fall.

His soul can open eyes that are shut tight.

His soul can be a caring pillow
on a troubled night.

His soul can be whatever you want it to be,

as his soul is deeply rooted in poetry.

PREFACE

What is poetry?

I define my poetry as reflections or expressions delivered through words.

This collection of poems has something for every reader.

We all go through things in life, be it heartache, broken relationship, or celebrations. Maybe you long for a word of encouragement or a laugh. Perhaps you need words to strengthen your faith, or you desire to rekindle a relationship, or want to light a spark of romance in your marriage or an ongoing relationship.

No matter what you need, look no further; I'm sure you can find solace here in my book, *The Soul of a Poet*.

May this book touch you and become an inspiration in your life. As you read one poem, may that poem keep your curiosity fueled to read the next and the next.

So, relax and allow these words to take you to a place of serenity where you feel *The Soul of a Poet*.

Poetically yours,

Ronald Marsh Smith

LOUD AND BOLD

LOUD AND BOLD

DON'T LOOK DOWN ON ME

You treat me as if I turn your stomach inside out.

Don't understand why it's me you negatively talk about.

I may not have designer clothes and expensive cars,

but my life has the most priceless gift, an everlasting star.

You see it's the star that keeps me from all harm and danger.

It's the star that led the Wise Men to the Holy Manger.

I don't have a clock that goes tick-tock to open my eyes,

but I do have a precious touch with a glorious sunrise.

It's shameful you prefer to treat me this way.

I've made much effort to be a friend to you every day.

So again, I ask you, please don't look down on me.

Because you never know; I could very well be the Christ from Galilee.

Loud and Bold

I STARE

As I look out my window and stare,

my mind wonders why I am not there.

I see the magnificent stars of the galaxy,

beautiful and huge I stare to find a place for me.

I stare to conquer my fears, heartaches, and pain,

things you wouldn't understand even if I explained.

LOUD AND BOLD

JAIL

Well, I tell you - life is pure hell,

especially when you live in jail.

An 8X10 cell is what is called home.

"Guard, I want to use the telephone."

I haven't received one piece of mail,

since I landed myself in jail.

Seems my family has forgotten me, my friends too.

Man, I tell you jail ain't for me, nor for you.

LOUD AND BOLD

STAINED GLASS

Everyone has a stained glass

that gives focus on the future and not the past.

Allow your stained glass to be a motivating kit,

to keep your engine primed so you won't quit.

There's a story behind a glass embedded with years of stains.

It's that story that can help someone else out the rain.

Keep the stained glass polished in your trophy case.

It was given to you, and it can never be replaced.

Your stained glass has gone through *a many* storm.

But it's God who has kept it in your heart where it is warm.

LOUD AND BOLD

WONDERING

I'm a million miles away from home,

wondering why I am so alone.

Wandering day and night,

in search of a glance of sunlight.

If you have ever seen a spinning wheel,

then you know just how I feel.

My *wondering* takes me further into time.

Desperately I search for peace of mind.

If I keep *wandering* the way I do

I'll have no life, not even you.

LOUD AND BOLD

YOUR BOOK

Everyone that has life has a book they can write,

sharing the fun and drama they experience from morning to night.

If one just sits down and take a look,

they will see they too are the author of a good book.

No need to be famous like the movie stars.

People want to read about just who you are.

Tell the story how your life came into motion,

about your ancestors that came across the Atlantic Ocean.

Please describe how you were as a little child.

Were you quiet and shy or were you running wild?

Did you ever have a childhood friend,

who promised to stay in contact until life's end?

Instead of reminiscing about your life in a mirror glass,

ink those memories into a book that'll forever last.

STORIES TO BE TOLD

A FAMILY CHRISTMAS

The birth of Christ should be in everyone's mind

as we are blessed to see Christmas time.

Trees are decorated with lights and bows.

Kids are laughing as they play in the snow.

Carolers strolling neighborhoods singing silent night

as stars in the sky shine soft and bright.

The fireplace illuminates a warm atmosphere.

Lovebirds snuggle as emotions smother the air.

Under the tree are boxes wrapped so beautifully.

A gentle voice asks, "Is there a gift for me?"

The radio plays old Christmas sounds,

while family members arrive from out of town.

Around the tree, we wrap up all the love and holiday cheer.

Together as a family, we pray God's blessings for a new year.

STORIES TO BE TOLD

CHRISTMAS TIME

Christmas is a magical time of a year;

family and friends come together to share laughter and cheer.

Christmas trees are decorated with lights that glow.

Outside, kids play in fresh fallen snow.

Ladies in the kitchen, mix species into an unforgettable meal.

While the men sit in front of a big screen, watching football thrills.

As eyes are gleaming excitement at the delicious dinner prepared,

hands are grasped together for a traditional family prayer.

The smell of eggnog refreshes the quiet atmosphere,

while lovebirds cuddle up like teddy bears.

As Christmas Day evolves into Christmas night,

among the stars is a full moon stunning and bright.

We give thanks to our Heavenly Father sitting above

for providing us a Christmas filled with happiness and love.

THANKSGIVING

Family and friends gather far and near,

celebrating the many blessings, they hold dear.

America flies the red, white, and blue.

Thanksgiving is a day that's sacred and true.

Tree limbs barely have a leaf in sight.

 Grounds are covered with leaves crisp and bright.

Thanksgiving is here, our minds have made a U-turn,

from what the past has taught us, to what we've learned.

We take our pleasure in material things,

forgetting the pleasure that family and friends bring.

In homes, you hear sounds of spoons doing a lot of *mixin',*

as generations of women are at work in Grandma's kitchen.

Grandma opens the oven to check the turkey as it bakes.

Out loud someone asks, "Who's fixing the chocolate cake?"

The table is spread with all the trimmings to eat.

Stories to be Told

Grandpa directs family and friends to take a seat.

A calm of peace overtakes the laughter and fills the atmosphere,

as family remembers loved ones, who are no longer here.

Instantly the dinner table comes to a quiet hush,

as family reflect on loved ones they miss so much.

Cherish and celebrate Thanksgiving each day,

for you'll never know when a friend or loved one will be taken away.

STORIES TO BE TOLD

MERRY CHRISTMAS BABY

The trees are glittering with snow.

Your eyes are gleaming stars I want you to know.

So many gifts under the Christmas tree.

There's a lovely one for you, especially from me.

Church bells ringing, choir angels singing;

so much joy Christmas time is bringing.

Little kids outside playing in the snowy cold weather,

as we snuggle around the fireplace holding hands together.

Kissing and holding each other tight,

thanking God, we're together on this chilly Christmas night.

STORIES TO BE TOLD

MERRY CHRISTMAS MY DEAR

Wishing you a Merry Christmas my dear.

With heartfelt love for us to have a prosperous New Year.

This time of year brings out the tender side of me.

Baby, let's go cuddle underneath the Christmas tree.

Better yet let's find a beautiful mistletoe,

where we can share a kiss nice and slow.

I love to see you stare at the Christmas tree sparkling lights,

'*cause* your face releases a smile so ravishing and bright.

While Santa makes his trip around the world,

I ask him to leave a present for my pretty girl.

As Christmas bring much laughter and cheer,

I want to say to you, "Merry Christmas, my dear."

FEELINGS OF FIRE

FEELINGS OF FIRE

DO MY

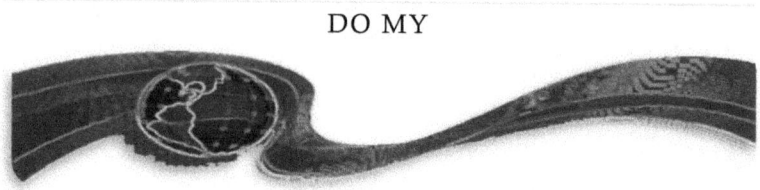

Do my love illuminate your heart,

Just as the moon does the dark?

Do my God-sent anointing of care,

reveal my promise, always to be there?

Do my smile arouse your emotions to quiver,

as your mind begins to wonder can I deliver?

Do my journey for your love catch wind and sail,

or do my feelings become an empty fairytale?

FEELINGS OF FIRE

LAST NIGHT

Oh, how I was hoping that you would call.

I held the phone under my pillow; to sleep I could not fall.

Patiently I waited for you to dial my line;

Waiting to share just what was on my mind.

Staring deeply into your eyes, looking at your beautiful face.

Deep in my heart, I desire a kiss as we embrace.

Our hands begin to slowly entwine;

feelings tick like a clock keeping time.

Touching your delicate, smooth skin

made me realize our feelings have become more than friends.

Kissing you is of so much pleasure.

You would forever be my keepsake treasure.

How can something wrong be so right?

These are the things I thought of, while I waited last night.

FEELINGS OF FIRE

PRETTY LADY

Pretty Lady, the tears won't stop escaping from my eyes.

Love for you is much stronger than I realize.

Pretty Lady, our time together is drawing near,

I drown in an ocean to hide my tears.

Pretty Lady, life as I know it shall never be the same,

upon my lips will always be your name.

Pretty Lady, in my arms I want you to fall asleep,

as I plant a million kisses on your tender cheek.

Pretty Lady, so badly I want to satisfy your moans,

and place you on a rose pedal throne.

Pretty Lady, I dream of us meeting at our special place,

so, we can release our emotions as we embrace.

Pretty Lady, don't think my feelings will fade away.

I've got them in my heart where they will eternally stay.

FEELINGS OF FIRE

YOUR EYES

Let me explore the mystery of your sensual eyes.

I want to find the truth, please no hidden lies.

Your eyes ignite a soft tender flame,

that will hopefully ease our hurt and pain.

Your eyes shine like a diamond carved into a pearl.

Girl, you can believe forever you'll be part of my world.

Your eyes give me the strength to endure this unpleasant storm.

It reflects a love that's powerful, yet so warm.

Your eyes are a star beaming millions of miles away,

keeping our path illuminated regardless of where we stay.

Allow me to hold you tight as I stare into your eyes,

planting kisses as we dream waking to the morning sunrise.

FEELINGS OF FIRE

PASSION FOR YOU

Our love of passion and desire

is protected by an eternal flame of fire.

Nothing can drive a wedge between us you see;

our relationship is special, and it's meant to be.

I want you to count on me as I count on you.

Together there is nothing we can't get through.

I think I'm going into cardiac arrest,

as I hear my heart pounding out of my chest.

May I serenade you as we stroll alongside a peaceful stream?

You are a beautiful lady gifted to satisfy all of my dreams.

Like a garden of flowers being showered with the morning dew,

I hope we awake together sharing the words, "I love you."

TRUTH AND DESIRE

TRUTH AND DESIRE

BLACK DIAMOND

Sparking black diamond clear as can be.

A creation by God to last throughout eternity.

Molded and shaped with curves signifying blessed.

Hips well defined absolutely tell the rest.

Never the same, not an ordinary design.

Sculptured with cuts that represent fine.

A spirit softly protects her Proverbs soul,

yet standing out just enough to show she's in control.

Her eyes will helplessly vaporize you into a melting pot,

sending out alarms that define she's hot.

Her emotions radiate a passionate fire,

deeply burning for one to admire.

TRUTH AND DESIRE

FROM MY HEART

From my heart, I will always have images of you,

images that shall cast out my darkest blue.

From my heart, you'll never be forgotten at all,

even though we both know our curtain is soon to fall.

From my heart, I will remember your lovely face,

and truly remember the times we exchanged a tender embrace.

From my heart, I will always talk to you,

and I hope and pray you'll still talk to me too.

From my heart will be a lasting love for you.

God knows I just don't know how I will make it through.

From my heart will be sincere feelings and emotions,

always rising up like the waves of the beautiful oceans.

From my heart, I can go to a place far away,

and pretend I love you each and every day.

TRUTH AND DESIRE

I DREAM

I dream when I look at the stars above.

I dream when you tell me of your love.

I dream as I go throughout the day's hour.

I dream when I see a beautiful flower.

I dream when I fall asleep at night.

I dream when I hold you tight.

I dream when I hear your tender voice.

I dream when you make me rejoice.

I dream when I'm happy and when I cry.

I dream when I laugh, I dream of saying goodbye.

I dream when I give you a kiss.

I dream of the time, days and years I'll miss.

I dream of our times together.

I dream of us snuggled forever.

And even if the dream can never come true.

I'll still go back and dream of you.

TRUTH AND DESIRE

IF I COULD

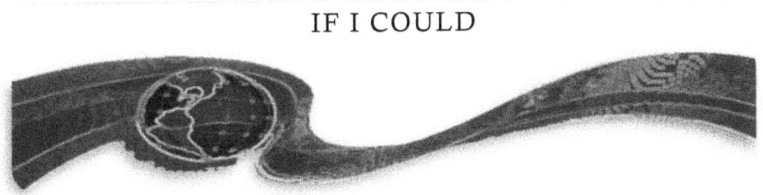

If I could send you a flower,

it would be sent every second of every hour.

If I could gaze into your stunning eyes,

I'd be there to dry your tender cry.

If I could hold your priceless hand,

I would engrave a love poem that will forever stand.

If I could only share a moment or two;

I want to have a sincere, loving conversation with you.

If I could love your mind, body, and soul,

I promise the memories of us shall be worth more than the world's silver and gold.

TRUTH AND DESIRE

LOVE IS

Love is like a hurricane wind,

blowing with no end.

Love is like a desert storm blast,

leaving scattered memories of the past.

Love is such a peculiar thing,

instead of hope, it can destroy your dream.

Love is like a sad love song,

it plays for a while then it's gone.

Love is supposed to be a bright spot for tomorrow,

releasing all pain and sorrow.

Love has placed in my eyes a blazing fire;

that my teardrops refuse to extinguish – yes, this is dire.

When I die, tears I will no longer cry,

and only you will know that love is the reason why.

TRUTH AND DESIRE

PLANTING LOVE

Let's plant a love garden and do how we choose,

cause you and I have nothing to lose.

I want to touch you until I find the spots,

that light your fire and keep you hot.

Soft music playing into your ears,

totally erasing all worries and fears.

Allow me to listen to your heartbeat tonight,

as I hold you oh so nice and tight.

Let the vibrations of our souls captivate into sexual feelings,

as our bodies begin to cling for sexual healing.

WISDOM AND TRUTH

WISDOM AND TRUTH

DEAR LORD

Dear Lord, I know You haven't heard from me in a while,

probably not since I was a little child.

But now here I am on my bended knees,

feeling ashamed but need to ask won't You help me, please.

My heart is broken into a million pieces, so much for life.

Dog ran away, also the woman who claimed to be my wife.

Please come to me sweet Amazing Grace.

Wipe away this life that's plentiful with disgrace.

Rebuild my life with a prayer fountain,

that will strengthen me to climb my troubled mountain.

Dear Lord, wash me up just one more time.

It's Your forgiveness I'm hoping to find.

For You said in Your word let Your will be done.

Lord, I give it all to Jesus, Your only begotten son.

WISDOM AND TRUTH

HEAVEN ISN'T FREE

People are looking forward to life after death in eternity,

but little do they know heaven's mortgage isn't free.

Remember Christ paid the ultimate cost,

to save His children who are lost.

It's written down in God's holy book,

just extract a recipe or two and begin to cook.

The ingredients may not taste good at first,

but keep using them because you'll begin to thirst.

The first step as your journey begins,

is to admit to yourself that you have sinned.

Now please don't think you can just sit back;

rest assured the devil is always on the attack.

The process is worth going through,

cause God has many blessings for you.

Just get down on those bending knees,

and say, "Lord, I stretch my hand to thee."

WISDOM AND TRUTH

Don't be discouraged, have patience and wait.

You can believe, the God we serve is never late.

The prescription has been written down for you;

it'll surely work if you only follow through.

Finally, if you truly want a piece of God's estate,

repent from your sins before it's too late.

WISDOM AND TRUTH

HOW MUCH DO I OWE YOU

How much do I owe you Lord for waking me up each day,

and getting me started along the way?

How much do I owe you Lord for putting food on my table,

and reminding me that You're truly able?

How much do I owe you Lord for putting clothes on my back,

with constant reminders to me to follow heavens track?

How much do I owe you Lord for protecting me, from all harm and danger,

always loving me even when I become a total stranger?

How much do I owe you Lord for your compassion and care,

never forsaking my requested prayer?

How much do I owe you Lord for loving me,

an unconditional love you carried to Calvary?

How much do I owe you, Lord, you've never sent me a bill to pay,

but in my heart, I owe you my life, my praises each and every day?

WISDOM AND TRUTH

MASTER

Master of every ocean and every sea,

I pray you watch over me.

My days are on this earth have kept me lonely.

Jesus, I turn to, for He's the one and only.

In this world one day we can be up, and the next we can be down.

One day I'm leaving to get to that sacred ground.

My mother will be there waiting for me

I thank the Lord for setting her soul free.

My father, sister, and brother will also be waiting there.

So, when I get home, we'll all have individual stories to share.

As I lift my hands for you to take me home tonight,

Lord, I ask you to guide me like a sparrow in flight.

When I reach those pearly gates marveled in gold,

I'll be able to sit down and rest my soul.

WISDOM AND TRUTH

NO GRAVE

Go tell the world and throughout the town,

no grave could keep my Savior down.

My time on earth is almost done.

Soul is bound for heaven; victory is won.

Real love of life is finally found,

standing on Christ's solid ground.

Every sin Christ has forgiven me.

Now I have peace and eternity.

Such a glorious day God has given me.

In my heart lives the living tree.

WISDOM AND TRUTH

NOBODY KNOW

Nobody know my anguish and sorrow.
Nobody know my prayers for a brighter tomorrow.
Nobody know the tears I refused to shed.
Nobody know the times I'd wish to be dead.

Nobody know the obstacles placed in my road.
Nobody know unless you heard the stories I told.
Nobody know my many fights.
Nobody know my sleepless nights.

Nobody know my life's turbulence and uproar.
Nobody know why God gave me wings like an eagle to soar.
Nobody know when God will rescind my stay.
Nobody know my time, hour or day.

Nobody know why I was blessed with so much favor.
Nobody know but my Lord and Savior.

WISDOM AND TRUTH

WHEN MORNING COME

Does it rise from the depths of my burden soul?

No, it rises from my Creator who has total control.

When morning come I prepare myself for the struggles at hand;

the struggles of my skin tone of being a black man.

When morning come I can't afford to linger in such pity and sorrow,

These two negatives can control one's destiny of not seeking to challenge tomorrow!

When morning come, fortunate am I to have another peek;

To glimpse the sun rays as it slowly awakens me out of much-preferred sleep.

When morning come God has empowered me to take another breath,

to go forward and give life what I have left.

When morning come.

ATTENTION TO YOUTH

ATTENTION TO YOUTH

CHILDREN OF THE NIGHT

We are children of the night,

trying to get it right.

We are young children of today,

hoping our parents show us the way.

We are children of all races,

hoping people don't judge us by our faces.

We are children seeking knowledge,

hoping one day to attend college.

We are children aiming toward a goal,

to help our society open their eyes that appear closed.

We are children of the night,

hoping we escape the dark and find the light.

We are children of the night,

not wanting to fight but wanting to do right.

ATTENTION TO YOUTH

DON'T HAVE A CLUE

Bout to finish school, don't have a clue

What in the world am I going to do?

Had no thoughts of taking the ACT.

Got no one to blame but poor *ole* me.

Seems like I belong in the lost and found.

Friends heading to college and I'm still hanging around.

Will somebody please help me, I don't have a clue,

on just what in this world I want to do.

Skipping school and hanging out at the malls having fun.

Messed around with a girl, nine months later now I have a son.

Being called dada, daddy or father don't appeal to me.

I got to get away and find my destiny.

Dragging jeans, hip-hop music, texting my boys is the thing.

Trying to be a father is the furthest from my dreams.

ATTENTION TO YOUTH

Will somebody lay life out to me, I need a plan.

I have a son; I got to grow up and take on the responsibilities of a man.

My parents have given up on me because I have no clue.

Now you tell me what a young man is supposed to do.

Got to get life together, got to get it right.

So, I can find a place for my girl and son to sleep at night.

I have got to come up with a plan quick and fast.

So, I can say I finally got myself together at last.

I got to ask God to please turn my life around,

before I end up buried six feet underground.

DREAMING

I am young, ambitious, strong and gifted.

Just need a little encouragement to stay lifted.

The world compass maps out many directions to turn.

I fight hard to remain in school and empower myself to learn.

Thanks to everyone who has invested a little time in me.

No worries, I will make you proud, you just wait and see.

A road map toward success is never the same,

but don't worry I won't bring you any shame.

While being physically and emotionally drained,

no one has taken the time to ask me to explain.

So, my eyes are focused on how I want my life to be.

Now please excuse me while I go dream, up under that beautiful shade tree.

ATTENTION TO YOUTH

I HAVE AUTISM

(Dedicated to Bennett)

I am a boy with autism, but I have dreams.

So, don't think I'm not going to be anything.

I am a boy with autism who can run and play.

And at night before I go to sleep, I always pray.

I am a boy with autism who is truly loved,

by my parents, family, and God above.

I am a boy with autism who is full of joy.

 Don't believe me, just buy me a new toy.

I am a boy with autism who has a loving heart.

I love riding in my daddy's golf cart.

I am a boy with autism learning the best I can,

so I can grow up to be a confident, strong man.

ATTENTION TO YOUTH

STOP THE BULLYING

Why do you insist on bullying me?

Do I sense you have a little jealousy?

Bullying people is horrible, and frankly, it's not right.

So, why do you always go looking for a fight?

How did bullying become part of your genes;

I'm sure you didn't come into this world being mean.

Together we grew up as the best of friends.

Remember the pact we made, friends to the end?

Seems to me you've forgotten about all this.

And now I'm on your bully list.

I've been nothing but a friend to you all these years

Now you think it's funny to inflict my life with fears.

Extra, extra, breaking news off the press,

your old buddy is sick and tired of this mess.

If you think you are all that tough,

ATTENTION TO YOUTH

guess what; enough is enough.

People have taken their life because of the likes of you.

You ought to be ashamed of the ugly things you do.

It's time to teach you a lesson or two.

And then you'll see that bullying is not the right thing to do.

ATTENTION TO YOUTH

WE TOO EXIST

Allow us to share with you the things in our heart that we feel.

Then you'll see our dreams are not fantasy; they are real.

For the time God gives us on this earth to live,

we too want the best that life has to give.

There're no intentions of us to lose our inspiring light.

We will stand and keep going and win our fight.

Understand the millennial generation is here, and we do exist.

And we're ready to show the world we are not a bunch of misfits.

People fail to realize we have dreams staring out of our eyes.

Like generations of the past, we too have a passion to rise.

When it sometimes rains, the wind will blow,

just like generations come and go.

So, the next time you look into a glass in search of the truth,

ATTENTION TO YOUTH

just keep in mind there's a new generation called millennial youth.

We pray everyone will be proud of us and take a look,

as we create and leave the next generation our history book.

ATTENTION TO YOUTH

WHAT DO YOU SEE

Pretty Black girl tell me what do you see?

I see my ancestors being shipped across the Atlantic Sea.

Pretty Black girl tell me what do you see?

I see my ancestors arriving in America being sold into slavery.

Pretty black girl tell me what do you see?

I see my ancestors on a plantation starting a family tree.

Pretty black girl tell me what do you see?

I see my ancestors pulling cotton

while the Master's wife drinks nice cold tea.

Pretty Black girl tell me what do you see?

I see my ancestors fighting to flee a whip that inflicts pain and misery.

Pretty Black girl tell me what do you see?

I see the Emancipation Proclamation setting my ancestors free.

Attention to Youth

Pretty Black girl tell me what do you see?

I see the Emancipation is not a true document for people of color like me.

Pretty Black girl tell me what do you see?

I see my momma working hard to make life better for me.

Pretty Black girl tell me what do you see?

I see the struggles and sacrifices;

Malcolm, Martin, and others went through for my equality.

Pretty Black girl tell me what do you see?

I see myself one day as an intelligent,

educated black woman making a difference in this world,

just as my ancestors did for me.

BUILT-UP WALL

BUILT-UP WALL

FIGHT WITH CANCER

Cancer has inched into your life nice and slow,

hoping to deliver the final blow.

Cancer is trying to give you an unwanted scare,

thinking you are just going to sit there.

Cancer's goal is to strike and kill,

but God has given you enormous will.

Invite cancer to meet you in the lion's den,

and tell yourself it's time to win.

Don't worry about the burning pain.

God will give you the willpower to sustain.

Push every second of your days and be strong.

Family and friends are not ready to say, "So long."

Remember as you continue this fight down the road,

friends and loved ones are there to help carry your load.

BUILT-UP WALL

A GLIMPSE OF TOMORROW

Tomorrow is merely a glimpse of a hope and a dream.

Nothing's important because it's yet to be seen.

Tomorrow is packed with plans one inspires to ignite,

only if God gives the blessing to see the morning light.

Tomorrow has no impact on how you live today.

If you have any hope, don't forget to pray.

Tomorrow holds the mystery key of an unknown town,

for nobody knows who's going to be around.

BUILT-UP WALL

A SMILE

A smile can take you a long way,

it can help erase the worries of yesterday.

A smile can massage a hurting pain,

it can bring sunshine to replace the rain.

A smile is a beautiful ray of light breaking through,

creating a place that is perfect for only you.

A smile can inspire people to have some hope,

as they climb down a slippery slope.

A smile can bring justice to the unjust,

to strengthen their faith to believe and trust.

A smile can take away those unwanted tears,

that has been carried around for *a many* years.

A smile is free; it doesn't cost anything to give,

it's an affection to inspire a troubled soul to fight and live.

A smile can release the greatest feeling called love,

it's the one thing that was started from God above.

BUILT-UP WALL

A VIEW OF LIFE

As the pendulum on the grandfather clock begin its side to side sway,

so, do memories of life slowly drift away.

While focusing on correcting life imperfections,

weights on the clock descended in one direction.

As life's viciousness deliver countless twist and turns,

it offers a chance to continue to learn.

Despite how life can accumulate years of struggle,

don't be scared and live life in a bubble.

If life brings a vapor of emotional sorrow,

be strong and know there is still a brighter tomorrow.

Life is measured in three phases: beginning, middle and end.

We all should know it's the middle that is the most important my friend.

BUILT-UP WALL

DIFFICULTIES

When difficulties of life take hold,

be determined and strong not to fold.

When the problems seem too much to bear,

believe someone is standing by and that they care.

Agony viciously grabs on you tight,

to remind you to get ready for a fight.

Long as you believe there's a light at the end of the road,

then you're destined to find your pot of gold.

Let faith be the substance to carry you through,

the difficulties that have lingered on you.

Time doesn't stand still so why should you.

since there's so much in life you want to do.

BUILT-UP WALL

DOWN BUT NOT OUT

Now that the devil has knocked you on the ground,

it's not too late to turn your life around.

May God bless you with a magnificent spiritual healing,

to replace that lonesome, broken feeling.

Surrender your all to God's amazing grace.

Allow His mercy to remove the sorry from your face.

Just have a little faith and believe,

that in time blessings of happiness you'll receive.

The devil has robbed you and got you on the wrong track,

now you've got a chance to redeem yourself and fight back.

As the winter season turns into beautiful spring,

know in your life God can and will do a new thing.

As the skies open from heaven above,

patiently God awaits with His everlasting love.

BUILT-UP WALL

I AM A SLAVE

In the midst of the night stolen and shipped across the ocean sea,

taken from my native Africa and my loving family.

As tears of anger submerge my face,

shackles and chains bound me in place.

Stripped and whipped like I have no pride,

this is a journey I wish to have died.

Placed on an auction block lost and confused,

body been beaten down and abused.

Bids of money are being screamed out for me.

Can't believe this is the land where all men are free.

Up at dawn to pick cotton in the blazing sun.

Moaning and singing spirituals until the day is done.

Often asking, "Is a brighter tomorrow heading my way?"

Cause in this life as a slave I can no longer stay.

BUILT-UP WALL

KINDNESS

Never forget to extend an act of kindness to someone today.

It could bring happiness to their lives in an unknown way.

A person could need a hug or a dollar or two,

just a touch of kindness to make it through.

To set judgment on one in desperate need just isn't fair,

for one day it could be you in despair.

Delivering kindness is something we all should understand.

Let's not be ashamed to lend a helping hand.

TOMORROW

(Inspired by my loving wife, Betty)

Tomorrow isn't promised to you nor me.

And yet plans are made as if it's a guarantee.

Tomorrow is a destiny you *hope* to find,

as clocks around you continue to wind.

Tomorrow is a world that stays at bay.

It's up to God to bless you to see another day.

Tomorrow is a mystery holding the unknowns to time,

controlling tomorrow is not within the power of mankind.

There's nothing wrong in making plans for tomorrow.

Just include your soul that God may choose to borrow.

If and when tomorrow comes and I'm not around,

rest assured my soul is heaven bound.

BUILT-UP WALL

TROUBLED

Troubled times have come into your life,

not as a mother, but as a wife.

Surely your marriage was built with love and trust.

So, staying in the fight is a must.

The obstacles before you - remember to knock them down,

so trouble doesn't engage you by leaps and bounds.

Your heart may be drooling with heartaches and pain,

God will give you the strength to sustain.

Regroup and clear the obstacles that stirred this up.

Let your man know you're still his delicious buttercup.

Make notes of what your soul is trying to unleash.

Pray into your marriage, and the devil will release.

Seek out choices that'll stop hurting one another,

and find solutions to bring back loving each other.

BUILT-UP WALL

Though you may think it's right or wrong, it's always God's call.

Remember, it's you and the family who will ultimately take the fall.

In your heart, please do not think it's worth it just to be right,

remember marriage is never worthy of a useless fight.

BEFORE YOU FALL

BEFORE YOU FALL

BURIED IN THE ATLANTIC OCEAN

A young boy asks, "What's all the commotion?"

Quietly a voice responds,

"I've been buried in the ocean for over a hundreds of years.

The ocean water has become my tears.

Had no intentions of this happening to me;

I was a little boy who was stolen from my family."

The young boy asks the voice in the sea,

"Explain to me just how could this all be."

An astounding number of voices reply, "You need to go learn your history.

There's *a many* of us beneath the ocean floor.

Some jumped because we had no intentions to see slavery's door.

A many died on the long, long journey ride.

The slave catchers threw them over the ship's side."

BEFORE YOU FALL

Voices from the ocean continued to say,

"This story is true, we have no reason to lie."

At that moment the young boy sorrowfully began to cry.

The boy then asks the voices, "Is there anything I can do?"

The voices reply, "Tell the world you know why

the Atlantic waters aren't a beautiful blue."

BEFORE YOU FALL

END THIS WAY

There's nothing neither one of us can do or say.

We both knew it would eventually end this way.

We can never be together like we once planned.

Now you're a lonely woman and I a lonely man.

Seems as if my life is now destined to be through,

as I count the days of missing you.

As we walk away promising not to ask why,

we should share one last kiss and say goodbye.

Never did I want to use the phrase, "We are through."

Believe me; I tried to be a good man to you.

But now I have no other choice.

Can't you hear the sadness in my voice?

Loving you gave me a new breath of life,

but honestly, made me realize I love my wife.

Please don't be mad and I don't want you sad.

Let's just remember and enjoy the moments we both had.

BEFORE YOU FALL

HELP ME

Life for me hasn't been a bed of roses,

trying to make something out my life before my living closes.

I don't need a bunch of sorrow and tears.

I've had enough of that to last a thousand years.

To laugh and say I am a waste and even a disgrace,

surely won't erase the hurt and anguish that sets on my face.

I need a lot more than your sympathy,

cause that's not going to help me.

Don't be ashamed to reach out to me;

God's going to bless you more than abundantly.

Have the courage and take a stand.

Be a blessing toward your fellow man.

As funny as this may seem,

I too am seeking the good old American dream.

LIFE

As you go down life's road of *a many* choices,

don't allow yourself to be spooked by unknown voices.

Make decisions that can only be satisfied within your soul.

Allow no one to take your life and spin it out of control.

Be who you want to be as you travel along the way.

Have no worries of tomorrow or the past of yesterday.

No one deserves to be disrespected whether standing or in the ground.

Life should be viewed great, despite its ups and downs.

Life is not designed to be a bed of roses.

Roses may be a onetime gift when your living closes.

LIVE LIFE

Life has its shares of ups and downs,

more than enough to go around.

Sometimes darkness will shadow your life,

dishing out plenty of headaches and strife.

During the pain and hardest trials,

remain faithful and hold to your smile.

Create in you a secret place wherein,

you find the power to rebut the devil's sin.

Live your life free and unafraid.

Remember this day the Lord has made.

TROUBLING TIMES

So, you feel like you're the laugh of the town,

your world has suddenly been turned upside down.

This disappointment has capsized your mind.

You long for peace, but it's useless to find.

Enjoying a good night sleep is hard to do,

because what has happened also affects you.

As you wait on one to step forward and explain,

your heart tells you, life will never be the same.

You carry pain and sorrow no one can see.

cause you have buried it deep and thrown away the key.

You wonder, *is it hate that keeps me whole?*

For you've buried all emotions deep inside your soul.

Faking happiness is nearly an impossible task;

you long for a home to tearfully remove your mask.

BEFORE YOU FALL

You call on the Lord more than ever now,

as you surrender your problems as you bow.

You ask to be molded into a woman of courage and grace,

with a Godly smile symbolizing the strength on your face.

BEFORE YOU FALL

VOWS BROKEN

Because the two of you refuse to stay,

your love slowly begins to wither away.

The vows of love you both took,

now are going to end up in the divorce book.

The both of you seem not even to care,

of the broken heart, the children will bear.

If you think the grass is greener on the other side,

be careful because someone has told you a lie.

Marriage is not designed to be a one-way street;

you should help one another stand firm on your feet.

When the rain of pain sticks around too long,

the two of you have got to come together and be strong.

BEFORE YOU FALL

What God brought together, let no one come in between,

because that's not what your marriage vows mean.

EYES SHUT TIGHT

EYES SHUT TIGHT

AT PEACE

(Rest in Peace: Joe McNeil, Jr.)

My dearest Mom and Dad,

I gave this earthly life my very best shot.

Much thanks because I know you gave me a lot.

Although God lent me to you for a short 45 years,

I ask that you not shed any more tears.

I know my death has brought much pain and sorrow,

but, never forget you taught me there's a brighter tomorrow.

Please don't worry; I felt not one inch of pain.

My passing was beautiful; it's impossible to explain.

Though my mortal body you have truly lost,

my soul rests with Jesus who paid the ultimate cost.

So, I pray you find comfort in knowing I'm okay.

Remember, one day you too will have to fly away.

Eyes Shut Tight

BRUNO

Bruno gave his love
in his own unique way:

his little bark, licking tongue
and his running around always wanting to play.

Never did Bruno ask for much,
he loved a tummy rub with a soft, gentle touch.

A little guy carrying a tough name, Bruno had more VIP
Class than Hollywood's fame.

Bruno's favorite things
he loved to do:
lick my feet, chew my sock and taking a walk
every morning around two.

Handpicked at Pass Pet Store
by my wife,
Bruno gave us 16 years, 11 months, and 9 days of his
precious tender life.

Now that Bruno has said goodbye,
I pray GOD takes care of him in the Heavenly sky.

Bruno, until we are reunited, I am going to miss you.
A locket of hair, pictures, and memories
are all I have to cling too.

Eyes Shut Tight

(Rest in Peace: My pet Yorkie)

EYES SHUT TIGHT

CAM

So sorry Cam had to leave you at such an early age,
but God asked him to become a member of Heaven's
Yorkie stage.

Always remember Cam in your own special way.
Oh please don't forget little Cam's birthday.

Remember Cam was your first ring bearer,
that made it official you two belong together.

Although it was just for a little while,
I'm sure in many ways Cam made you both smile.

Never forget how Cam loved his fun-filled and exciting
walks,
and please don't forget Cam's personal one on one talks.

So, remember when you sit on the sofa by the door,
your buddy Cam still sits calmly in your lap or on the floor.

Know that Cam will always be your four-legged friend.
He loved you from the beginning until the very end.

It's okay to get another companion, Cam is at peace with
it all.

Cam is bragging to God that with you, he was blessed and
had a ball.

Eyes Shut Tight

(Rest in Peace: My son and daughter-n-law's pet Yorkie)

EYES SHUT TIGHT

I AM FREE

(Rest in Peace: Tiffany Davis)

Cancer,

my body you took total control,

but just know God Almighty has rights to my soul.

My body inside appeared to be a mess,

but within my soul, I still felt blessed.

You crept up on me like a thief in the night,

didn't give me a fair chance to fight.

You released your poison into my body awfully quick,

didn't understand why or how I became your pick.

My dearest husband and loving son,

shed no tears of sorrow

I want you to live for what's left of the day and coming tomorrow.

As a family I know we still had a lot of places we wanted to see

EYES SHUT TIGHT

But God made a decision to give me a ticket to be free.

I don't want your lives to be full of misery and rain,

So, let me be free from this heartache and bodily pain.

Remember in this life there's no logic to rhyme or reason,

so, until we see each other again, I want both of you to enjoy your season.

Now that my journey has come to an end and I say, "So long,"

Boris,

never forget the words to our favorite songs.

I will forever and ever be by your side,

like I was when you asked me to be your bride.

Although I only was able to give you 26 years of my life,

so proud was I to be your loving wife.

And to my son I want you to know,

I gave you birth and watched you grow.

I know God has created for you a perfect plan,

that'll truly turn you into a remarkable man.

And as I watch you from the Heavens above,

Eyes Shut Tight

In your heart will beat every ounce of my love.

Family and friends,

have no worries and have no fears

I think we all realized my time was near.

Never ever forget February 17th, 2017 when I rose

I said goodbye to my mortal life as it came to a final close.

EYES SHUT TIGHT

MISS YOU SIS

(Rest in Peace: Desiree Miner)

Family hearts are empty and broken forever.

In time our lives will eventually come back together.

You were my trusted confidante and best friend,

on whose loving support I could always depend.

Not seeing your beautiful, smiling face seems so wrong.

It's hard standing here trying to remain strong.

Despite your dreams and plans of things you still wanted to do,

God needed somebody in Heaven who is as special as you.

Without you, our lives will never be the same.

God called you home with a soft whisper of your name.

Away from the voices of those who you adore,

I realize Almighty God called you to that distant shore.

EYES SHUT TIGHT

Now that you have earned your heavenly wings and taken flight,

I am sure God will take care of you each and every night.

You'll always be around, overflowing us with love,

giving us strength, keeping us close as you watch from above.

My heartfelt prayer is one day I will see you as before,

beckoning me to come to join you on that lovely distant shore.

EYES SHUT TIGHT

MY BROTHER

(Rest in Peace: Roderick M. Smith)

Like lightning in the sky,

he was fast as a fly.

Running track was his game.

Achieving top honors was his fame.

Cool he was with class and style.

Everyone knew he was proud.

Hustling up pennies my brother did,

because he knew that was his only gig.

Enjoying life, he did try,

but he knew one day he too would die.

Dope he tried to use,

but he got abused.

EYES SHUT TIGHT

Fighting in bed for life my brother tried,

but God took him away to the beautiful sky.

Cool in the casket my brother laid,

for he never was worried or afraid.

My Brother, My Bad Ass Brother

Eyes Shut Tight

SHE'S WITH YOU

(Rest in Peace: Teresa Sales)

There's no way a grown man is supposed to cry,

but when Teresa died tears streamed from your eyes.

Thirty-two years of feelings and emotions wrapped up inside,

came out of you from nowhere like an ocean tide.

So much hurt and pain came into your life,

I'm sure you asked the Lord why you had to lose your wife.

Family and friends know you loved her from the depths of your soul,

and you're feeling your life is spinning out of control.

You sit in an empty house all alone,

just waiting for her spirit to come home.

She was your world and her presence you'll forever miss.

I'm sure you're asking God, "Can I have just one more kiss?"

Eyes Shut Tight

In your voice, I hear your broken heart as it continues to ache.

Just know God will see you through, however long it takes.

God didn't bring you this far for an unknown reason.

He's going to bless you into a new season.

Know Teresa has found a better life,

no more sickness, headache, and strife.

I'm sure she's is in Heaven looking down on you,

Saying, "Benny keep living for this is what I expect you to do."

THE MIGHTY NINE

(Rest in Peace: Charleston South Carolina Firefighters)

June eighteenth two thousand and seven,

is the day nine souls floated off to Heaven.

That day will forever be engraved into Charleston South Carolina's mind.

This was the day we lost firemen, not one or two but a Mighty Nine.

A ball of blazing fire came from nowhere.

Our firefighters stood strong and fought the fire flares.

The strength and courage it took as the Mighty Nine stood tall.

Into the building to save lives, not knowing the roof would fall.

Such a courageous act and unselfish devotion.

has brought much pain and sadden emotions.

The heartaches the families and friends must now bear,

as the days and years go by and their firemen are no longer there.

Eyes Shut Tight

Over one hundred thirty years of service the Mighty Nine gave.

Can you imagine the number of fires they fought and lives they saved?

Peace of mind will now be hard to find.

Never shall we forget Charleston's Mighty Nine.

The fire put the families in a tragic and devastating situation.

So many tears of sorrow, grief, and much aggravation.

Charlestonian's let us give the Mighty Nine a heartfelt salute,

and create a cherished memorial as an everlasting tribute.

They gave their lives; they passed the ultimate test.

Now God Almighty will give them a much-deserved rest.

PILLOW ON A TROUBLED NIGHT

ALWAYS LOVE YOU

Despite what you and I do,

I will always love you.

Truly I don't wish you any pain in your life.

A many days and nights I wonder why,

we're not husband and wife.

To always love you is to forever care about you girl.

I'm so glad for the moments you brought into my world.

When I say the words, "I'll miss you," every word is true;

though I haven't quite figured out,

just what I am going to do.

I pray our emotions and feelings won't lack any respect.

Either way, it goes, I'll always love you with no remorse or regret.

Always listen to the strings of my violin play.

I'll always love you more than my heart will ever say.

Pillow On A Troubled Night

CRIED MY LAST TEARS

I cried my last tears over you.

Just want to tell you we are through.

Thought what we had would last a lifetime,

but now dealing with you has blown my mind.

After playing your immature games,

my heartbeat is no longer the same.

Conversations with you are like a dual match.

Our relationship is so far gone it can't be patched.

There is absolutely nothing you can say or do,

to dissolve the heartache, you've put me through.

I've pulled myself together and dried my tearful eyes.

Finally, I have the strength to tell you goodbye.

Pillow On A Troubled Night

LIES OF LOVE

Are you in search of a love that is complimented with affection,

destined to take a relationship in the right direction?

Despite the size of the attractive diamond ring,

true love is a thing many can only dream.

Love is built with hard work from two.

Don't start it if it's not for you.

Love can bring on so much hurt that it can kill,

especially if one is climbing up another hill.

Love can treat you as if you're not there,

and leave you feeling that no one really cares.

Some take love as an outright game,

having no feelings and showing no shame.

Be on your P's and Q's and be wise,

not to get caught up in a web of lies.

PILLOW ON A TROUBLED NIGHT

REMEMBER

When you get old, more beautiful with hair of gray

Just reflect on the good times we had, during our day.

Remember how you and I got started,

and please remember the way we parted.

Remember the times on the phone

And don't forget the days, when we were alone.

Remember how we use to share a kiss,

for this is something, I will dearly miss.

Remember the laughter and the many tears.

Oh, please don't forget I said I'd Love you for the rest of my years.

Remember our times in the shower.

And don't forget all the lovely flowers.

Remember how we made each other feel.

The love was oh so real.

Remember we had our time,

PILLOW ON A TROUBLED NIGHT

but always know with me your heart will forever be mine.

Remember the words forever and a day.

These words are true until my life is finally taken away.

PILLOW ON A TROUBLED NIGHT

TIME

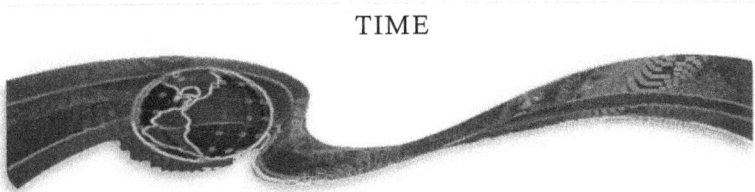

It's funny how the vapor of time slips away,

only to leave memories of faded yesterday.

Time couldn't get us beyond being the closest of friends,

leaving you to imagine what life together could have been.

But time refuses to let you share just how you feel.

Makes you wonder if time dealt you a raw deal.

As you unlocked years of feelings out of the box,

nothing was able to stop time from still going tick-tock.

Feelings are tucked away and hidden in one's heart,

where no one can ever rip them apart.

As years slowly continue to pass, time doesn't care.

Leaving a statement that time has been so unfair.

WISH

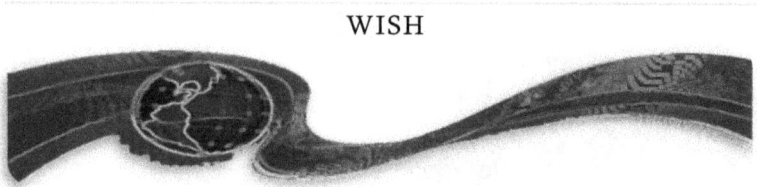

Wish we could go back and try again

But at this stage of life, neither of us would win.

What we once had was special and pure.

I know you loved me, of this I am sure.

Our relationship was agreed upon by both of our voice,

but you chose to separate and left me no choice.

I have no ill feelings, I love you just the same.

And I hope one day we can sit down, so you can explain.

WHATEVER
YOU WANT
IT TO BE

WHATEVER YOU WANT IT TO BE

MONA'S YARN

(Dedicated to Mona Wilson)

Relaxed, she sits working her needle hooks.

Bringing to life a pattern worth a thousand looks.

Carefully whipping yarn to the worlds no end,

creating gifts for strangers, family, and friends.

Stretches of yarn she releases gently from her hand,

to continue crocheting the creation she has planned.

She crochets in the evening until the wee hours at night,

ensuring every inch of yarn is nice and tight.

Her attitude may be abrupt as if she doesn't care,

but through her yarn, there's a loving heart there.

Her talent surely comes from the unknowns above.

Each piece is stitched together with such tender love.

WHATEVER YOU WANT IT TO BE

Her crochet of colors is such a rare treasure.

The cost of a stitch is hard to measure.

Row after row represents a story of its own,

like music notes setting a beautiful melody tone.

As each stitch of yarn come together, a story begins to unfold.

Mona's yarn is a beauty to behold.

WHATEVER YOU WANT IT TO BE

MY FINAL DAY

(A Personal Reflection)

A date and time will be recorded when I take my final breath.

This will confirm the last stage of life known as death.

Loved ones and friends will ask that legendary question, "Why?"

The answer is simple, for God determine it was my time to die.

I enjoyed my time on this precious earth,

since October 23, 1958, which is my recorded birth.

God blessed me with many fruitful years,

so please don't no one dare shed any tears.

It was not my wish for my life to expire.

The death Angel whispered it's me the Heavenly Father desire.

Surely, I didn't live my life as a scripted commercial.

I stated many times, "Life is not a rehearsal."

As I accept my final day for what it's worth,

Whatever You Want It To Be

let it be known my life had its ups and downs on this earth.

The good and bad I always cherished,

as for you, enjoy the memories cause one day you too will perish.

I have a one-way ticket for my final train ride.

Hopefully, it's on the track toward Heaven where I'll open my eyes.

Don't need no weeping filled with pity and sorrow.

Just know I have journeyed into a new tomorrow.

WHATEVER YOU WANT IT TO BE

NO ROSES

(A Personal Reflection)

Don't think about covering my casket with roses,

on the day my journey in life closes.

Best believe if I was okay living down here,

surely, I will be alright up there.

Stop it now, no need to shed tears of sorrow.

I'm gone, but you still have tomorrow.

So, don't sit there feeling sorry for me,

because you can best believe I am free.

WHATEVER YOU WANT IT TO BE

YOUR CALLING

*(Dedicated to Pastor Joe & Sis Sarah McNeil
Trinity Missionary Baptist Church, Goose Creek, SC)*

You tussled with God, yet knowing you were in an unwinnable fight.

God said, "I've chosen you to preach my word day and night."

No need for you to be afraid of your calling,

lean on Him, who is able to keep you from falling.

Remember what Sarah said with tears in her eyes,

"It's not my place to question God but Joe, please tell me why?"

God said, "Joe go forth and listen to what I say.

Know that Sister Sarah will be with you every step of the way."

Just as Moses led the people and parted the Red Sea,

God has chosen you to preach their souls free.

A many sinners are out there to be saved,

and in the church folks misbehave.

WHATEVER YOU WANT IT TO BE

You look for a strengthening word or two,

to deliver to the congregation that is waiting on you.

God says, "Words for you, I will provide."

Now go forth and don't you hide.

When you are smothered with problems, heartaches, and pain,

know God provides a rainbow after the rain.

When the calls and visits with the sick are too much to bear,

know the word of God is always there.

In the midnight hour, when you're troubled and all alone,

just fall upon your knees to seek God who sits on the throne.

May your journey be filled with blessings without end.

Continue to preach God's word and don't you bend.

"Who wants to be a pastor," you've asked again and again.

The Lord has spoken and said, "Lo, I am with you until the very end."

As you listen to the hymn, *The Lord will make a way somehow,*

know God has work in the vineyard so keep your hands to the plow.

WHATEVER YOU WANT IT TO BE

YOUR MARRIAGE

(Dedicated to Ryan & Monique Smith)

The two of you started your marriage journey a year ago,

before God, family, and friends in the city of San Antonio.

Both brought a mixture of ingredients to create a life,

that would acknowledge both of you as husband and wife.

In sickness and health until death do us part,

are words the two of you exchanged from the heart.

After the honeymoon, the work began,

to figure out how to create a marriage plan.

Ding, ding, now its round two.

Have the both of you savored enough love to make it through?

Remember marriage is not a toy bought game,

without teamwork a marriage can ignite into unbearable flames.

WHATEVER YOU WANT IT TO BE

Identify and commit to your destiny together,

making promises to survive the stormy weather.

Remember to say, "I'll love you through the think and the thin.

It's you and me baby to the dying end."

What God has brought together allow no one or nothing to wedge apart,

cause, in the long run, it will leave both of you with a broken heart.

Wanting to quit and just walk away,

is a cop out too many relationships encounter every day.

So, reminisce on why you said the infamous words, "I Do,"

and strive to strengthen one another to follow through.

DEEPLY ROOTED IN POETRY

A DADDY'S MESSAGE

Words of love I lack to share,

but know that Daddy truly care.

Though my conversations are very few,

still, I have plenty of love for you.

Sharing feelings may be hardly seen,

but don't ever think that daddy is mean.

Daddy might not be home before you go to bed,

understand I'm working hard to get the family ahead.

Fulfillment of your dreams is what I aspire for you,

Daddy will give his all to help them come true.

As you explore life and travel down an unbalanced road,

Daddy's here to help carry the load.

You need not harbor or wrap yourself in unwanted fear.

Daddy will always protect the ones he loves so dear.

DEEPLY ROOTED IN POETRY

If you begin to slip off a mountain that you want to climb,

know that Daddy is here to provide you with a lifeline.

A MOTHER'S KISS

As life is born and death takes it away,

a mother's kiss is a symbol of love that will forever stay.

Just as Pharaoh's army was swallowed deep beneath the red sea,

a mother's kiss is a golden treasure that will always be.

A mother's kiss can penetrate your soul like a soft-spoken word.

It can carry a melody like a beautiful mockingbird.

When you think your life is cluttered with sorrow,

remember a mother's kiss can brighten your tomorrow.

Don't let your mother's departure get you down.

If you have her kiss, she'll forever be around.

A mother's kiss will carve deep into your soul,

which you will forever treasure and gently hold.

Just remember the light along with the reflections of her past,

Deeply Rooted in Poetry

will seal her memories and kiss into an eternal looking glass.

FAMILY REUNION

(Dedicated to the Pace Family)

Let us go back from whence we came.

Back to Africa is where we'll discover our true family name.

Our ancestors were stolen and seeded throughout this Georgia land,

where we freely come together for our Family Reunion joining hand in hand.

Bondage and family separation our ancestors endured for hundreds of years.

Their struggles torched inspiration, hope, and strength into an undying tear.

Reminisce our past, enjoy the present, for the future we continue to pray.

And together as a family, we shall rejoice on our Family Reunion Day.

Women in the kitchen mixing generations of recipes in pots and pans,

as little girls' eyes gleam watching and wanting to lend a helping hand.

DEEPLY ROOTED IN POETRY

The smell of Grand Daddy's barbeque sauce smothers the air.

Hey, look on the porch, there's Grandma's old rocking chair.

Our young generation begin blasting the hip-hop sounds,

while the old school generation play Motown oldies that'll forever be around.

As our reunion festivities end and we go our separate ways,

let's not forget, it is our Ancestors that made this our Family Reunion Day.

FAMILY & FRIENDS

Today I'm here speaking with all of you,

reminding you God created a family that started with two.

Have you asked the question of why God created Family & Friends?

Is this something you'll ponder until your life end.

Let your life take shape in his hands,

for God Almighty indeed has the master plan.

Family & Friends are people who are meant to have a care.

And if in need they will surely be there.

They'll come to your rescue despite the time of day,

doesn't matter how close or the distance far away.

It's the care and love Family & Friends try to show,

just as Christ did for us so many thousand years ago.

Such a feeling of love sometimes is hard to describe.

You can see the appreciation as a soft tear fall from the eye.

DEEPLY ROOTED IN POETRY

Family & Friends are those who listen without a judging bone,

just as our Heavenly Father does as He sits on the throne.

Love and compassion are two things one ought to share,

to let Family & Friends know just how much you care.

Continue to love yourself, your Family & Friends,

and God will surely bless you until the very end.

SINGLE MOTHER

This is about a woman strong and bold,

so sit back and let the story be told.

She's a single mom who walks with pride,

for she'll tell you she has nothing to hide.

She's taken life accepting the bitter with the sweet,

knowing God has kept her standing on her feet.

As a single mother, raising not one but two.

In her heart, she knew what she had to do.

Working hard giving the job her utmost best,

returning home to work some more, having very little rest.

She set her goals high for her children to see,

that their mom's strength is rooted like the famous Angel Oak tree.

Deeply Rooted IN Poetry

Her time is spread amongst family and friends.

We all know she's there with us through thick and thin.

Yet she finds the time to reconnect her soul.

With her gracious Heavenly Father who's always in control.

EPILOGUE

I have often been asked, how can you just put words together like that? Well, several things come to mind. First, I experienced valleys in my life at a very early age. These life experiences provided some of the subject matter I have used when putting pen to paper. Poetry was an avenue for me to express my feelings. I'm writing about journeys I walked. I believe everyone has gone through or will go through negative as well as positive experiences in life. If you feel you haven't, just keep living.

Second, is that four letter word called love. Love is a wonderful thing when it's intact, but oh the pain and misery when it's not. During my early Army days, guys called me *The Poet* and would come to see me to solve their love problems by writing a poem to fit their individual need or situation. It was easy for me to do by putting myself in their situation, after hearing their problem. The words would flow.

My poetry tells stories about a journey that has challenged me from my childhood. The greatest achievement is when I can create a poem to help someone else get through their trials or tribulations. The 'Eyes Shut Tight' section of this book reflects the journeys of others when they needed some words written to ease their pain, put a smile on their face or a laugh back into their life. The Soul of a Poet has an inspiring message for all its readers.

So, find your place of tranquility and allow *The Soul of a Poet* to speak to you.

Everyone has a soul, but no one has the soul of this poet. Enjoy!

Ronald Marsh Smith

FOR MY HUSBAND

Never Give Up

As I was pondering what to write, two thoughts came to mind: *who* is this man and *what* a man. Well, he is Ronald Marsh Smith, a loving husband of more than thirty-five years and a father of three wonderful children. A man that will give you the shirt off his back, a man who doesn't mind taking time to give you personal advice on life, because he has a story of his own life's ups and downs that can be shared.

Watching Ronald pen his life's journey through his poetry, I'm reminded that he has a lot to give and I can truly see that he does have *The Soul Of A Poet*.

Each poem is carefully carved from a heart that reveals a personal message from the soul of **this** poet.

Thanks, Ronald, for these three words that you have drilled into me, our sons and everyone you have come in contact with, NEVER GIVE UP! It is a great honor that I salute my wonderful husband for a job well done.

Love Betty,

*And the Lord answered me: Write the vision;
make it plain on tablets, so he may run who reads it.*
(Habakkuk 2:2, NIV)

THE SOUL OF A POET

FOR MY WIFE

Forever My Love

As rivers flow into the oceans and seas,
so does our love grow strong and tenderly.

My Island of Paradise, my priceless ruby,
diamond and gold,
my fairy tale story I will forever hold.

I remember the day and hour
you swept me off my feet,
with your vibrant but gentle heartbeat.

Your eyes breathe energy into my life,
so blessed to have chosen you to be my wife.

The depths of the ageless seas
don't compare to measuring my love for thee.

The untiring waves of the ocean
can't describe my feelings or emotions.

I hold my head with so much pride
as you walk by my side.

Forever you are my days and my misty nights, always
illuminating our paths
with soft candlelight.

Love, Ronald

THE SOUL OF A POET (AUTHOR'S BIOGRAPHY)

Ronald Marsh Smith is a native of Cleveland, Ohio, and a retired US Army, Master Sergeant. Ronald Marsh Smith is a native of Cleveland, Ohio, and a retired US Army, Master Sergeant. Mr. Smith and his wife Betty have been married for more than 35 years. He is the loving father to three sons Ronald Jr, Raymond Sr. and Ryan.

Mr. Smith has a Bachelor's Degree in Professional Studies from Austin Peay State University, Clarksville, Tennessee. He is retired from Federal Government Service where he served more than fifteen years. Mr. Smith is a motivational speaker and when invited, works with students at Cross High School JROTC, Cross, SC.

He has also taught Sunday School and Vacation Bible School at his church, Trinity Missionary Baptist Church, Goose Creek, SC. He is an inspired writer of poetry. In 1996, Mr. Smith was awarded The National Library of Poetry Editor's Choice Award for Outstanding Achievement in Poetry.

Since the age of 2, Mr. Smith has overcome many trials in his life.

When asked what inspires him to write, he says, "life."

Truly having the soul of a poet, Ronald Smith offers the following observation:

"We've all had ups and downs, either from broken relationships, pain, and sorrow, or problems that life presents. If this hasn't been your experience," the author says, "just keep living. If my poetry can offer someone a bit of hope and inspiration, it's worth writing another poem and another poem and another poem."

In Spite of the Odds

In spite of the odds that spelled defeat,
you managed to stay on your feet.

In spite of the odds that makes one narrow & small,
you have grown wide with pride and stand very tall.

In spite of the odds that can misdirect one's plans,
you held steadfast and became a man.

In spite of the odds that can change a life,
you grew into manhood and took a wife.

In spite of the odds that spell success,
you have come through with the very best.

Ronald M. Smith's Aunt Murt (now deceased) summed up the poet in this personal poem she wrote and read at his retirement dinner from the US Army in July, 1998.

REVIEWS

REVIEWS OF RONALD M. SMITH POEMS

Upon reading the poems written by Ronald M. Smith I was instantly inspired. The poems bring motivation and instantly connects you to his feelings and how he thinks. The poems can be used to encourage. They are simple reminders that you can do anything you set your mind to regardless of the situation. Believe in yourself or no one else will.

Raymond & Toni Smith

Mildenhall Air Force Base, Suffolk England

I made an American flag wreath for competition in our local fair. It was the first crocheted piece I ever entered. It won 1st place and Best in Show. I gave it to Ron for Christmas, and he gave me a poem about my yarn. He was able to capture the beauty of my art with his art. His poem *Mona's Yarn* means as much to me as the blue ribbons I've won for my craft!

Mona L. Wilson

Summerville, SC

Reviews

This poem makes me reflect on the life, memories, and love I shared with Teresa for 32 years. The poem inspired me not to give up when I had the thoughts to do so. I would think about her and feel so sad, empty and lost. But I remembered the words from the poem, Teresa would want me to "keep living." For one day, I will be with her again, when it's all said and done.

Bennie Sales

Hampton, VA

If used correctly, words have the power to uplift, encourage, bring peace, give hope, and even ignite a flame. Words can paint beautiful pictures that cause your imagination to dance. Ronald's words do all of that and more. Enjoy!

Lashawna Bryant

Summerville, SC

The Soul of a Poet is a unique read and captures its audience with the many different relatable categories. The two poems that are dear to my heart are titled *Cam and Ronald III*. The poem *Cam* speaks such innocence of a dog that kept a smile on our faces and surely did

Reviews

enjoy his long walks. The poem highlights the good moments and happiness he brought into our lives. The clever wording in this poem brings his personality to life. The poem *Ronald III* speaks about our firstborn, and truly brings in the anticipation we had over the waiting months to meet our bundle of joy. The poem is beautifully written and brings tears of happiness to my eyes as I read it and make the realization of what a God sent blessing our first son has been to us. The Soul of a Poet brings you through many different emotions and has beautifully touched the lives of so many already. I highly recommend this book.

Ronald Jr. & Brittany Smith

Cypress, Texas

The poem "Heaven Isn't Free" inspired me! I was in the army myself, and I know that there is a price to pay for freedom. The poem was very witty and encouraging for me, especially knowing that the person who wrote that poem also served our country. May God bless all of our veterans!

Michael Oglesby

Parrish, Florida

REVIEWS

The poem, *I am free*, were words of encouragement to my son and I. Ron's interpretation of what my wife and sons' mother could have left us with, touched our hearts and gave us the strength to see that cancer may have taken over her body, but not her soul.

Boris Davis

Clarksville, TN

"I Am Who I Am"

This poem was dedicated to me, and it is definitely a true portrayal of me. I could not have described myself any better. Thank you, Ronald, for your positive perception of me.

"A Mother's Kiss"

This poem is a true portrayal of the feelings one should have for a mother. It describes the many things that a mother represents. Ronald, you did a great job of describing how a mother will always be a part of your life. I thank you for the poem "A Mother's Kiss" in memory of *my* mother.

Reviews

"A Daddy's Message"

This poem explains the role of a father and the sacrifices he makes. There are many times when a father is absent from the child's events because he is trying to make a better life for his family. The poem paints a picture of reassurance to the family that a father's love will always be there, even though he is not always there in person. Thank you, Ronald, for your insight into fatherhood.

Colette D. Ragins

Akron, OH

"A Mother's Kiss" reminds me of the poignant unconditional love, loss, hope, faith, and redemption found in the book of Ruth (in the Bible). The author was able to weave the connection between a mother and child in such a way that when all else is gone, the indelible mark left by 'a mother's kiss' leaves an indelible mark etched in the child's soul. Regardless of adversity, the "memories" of the kiss is untouchable.

Viola Smalls

Goose Creek, SC

Reviews

The realistic poems made me smile, think and some even made me frown. This is a masterpiece of poetry that will touch your heart and soul.

Felicia Gaston

Goose Creek, SC

Each poem tells a story from beginning to end—and still manages to rhyme. Simple words, carefully chosen to draw you effortlessly into complex thought—from the many journeys in this life.

Each poem paints a vivid picture in the reader's mind as seen from the writer's eye. And they also evoke the emotion from the writer's experience and clearly expresses the author's interpretation.

You will (I) leave each poem feeling as though you've (I've) had a conversation with the poet, yet never having spoken with him. Easily read, and deeply understood.

Comforting, relatable, provoking.

Vicky Lloyd

Dallas, TX

REVIEWS

"Rome & Rya"

Beautifully written poems about our son and daughter. The poems left us feeling speechless, delighted and loved. Can't wait for the book!

Ryan & Monique Smith

Stafford, VA

"I Have Autism"

The writings of Mr. Smith's poetry are truly from his soul. There is something for everyone in his poetry. The poem that was written about my grandson truly touched me dearly.

Robin Anderson

Summerville, SC

The poem, "Family Reunion" may cause some to wonder how our ancestors made it. My thoughts are they prayed and had faith in God. The poem highlights a journey from yesterday's struggles to a freer today.

Marvin L. Pace | Sergeant Major, U.S. Army, Retired

Stockbridge, GA

REVIEWS

The Soul of A Poet by Ronald Marsh Smith

"And we know that all things work together for good to them that love God, to them who are called according to his purpose."
Romans 8:28

The wait is finally over; God has truly blessed Mr. Ronald Marsh Smith with the gift of the spoken word! He pours his heart and SOUL into all of his work.

It's impossible to choose a favorite poem by Mr. Smith:

Brown Skin Dream, Good Morning My Love, Stormy Marriage, & Gloria Jean Lee.

Each poem draws you in and allows you to stand still in the moment. The inviting visuals, emotions, and aromas are so real!

Mr. Ronald M. Smith provides a true reading experience.

REVIEWS

Mr. Smith's Soul of A Poet is brave and exposes the vulnerable side of a strong, courageous man who is inspired by his beautiful and loving wife, Mrs. Betty Smith.

Congratulations to Ronald & Betty Smith for a job well done. Truly Gifted, and Blessed, need I say more?

Love Your Cleveland, Ohio Family:

Charles & Gloria Jean Lee,

Pearl Lee, Letha Lee, and Charles H. Lee Jr.

In Memory of Mommie:
Mrs. C. Elizabeth Berry

May God continue to bless and keep you and yours!

We love you!

A NOTE FROM THE PUBLISHER

As an avid reader, author and publisher, I have encountered many writings, fellow authors, and clients for whose work I am a fan. I love literature because it not only entertains, informs and inspire, it can also offer you access for what you may need.

For example, if you're lonely, you can find friends between the pages of any Terry McMillan book. If you're sad, you can find solace amidst the words penned by Sarah Young. And if romance is what you're seeking, one of my new discoveries is Francine Rivers. Yes, literature in most any genre can sate most any feeling one can imagine.

However, in my opinion, few books/authors can leave you changed.

The Soul of A Poet is definitely a book that will take you back to a place you remember fondly and it can also offer hope and a desire for someplace you haven't been. Truly, you'll never be the same again.

I admire Mr. Smith's command of his poetic talent. Not only does he have *the soul of a poet*, but his writings are prophetic in nature. He can pen a poem in minutes capturing the very emotion you were desperately seeking!

Mr. Smith has his pen on the pulse of the people and delivers a body of work that is sound, sensual, and sensitive.

Congratulations Mr. Smith on a job well done. Thank you for allowing us to assist you in presenting your work to the world!

Iris M. Williams

Author/Publisher

"We Believe In Your Dreams"

Iris M. Williams

Butterfly Typeface Publishing

PO Box 56193

Little Rock AR 72215

info@butterflytypeface.com

www.ingramcontent.com/pod-product-compliance
Lightning Source LLC
Chambersburg PA
CBHW071717090426
42738CB00009B/1796